MW00955326

My

MacBook Air

(M1,2020)

User's Handbook

An Essential Guide to Mastering How to Use the
New MacBook Air with M1 Chip + Tips and
Tricks on the macOS Big Sur 11

Chris Jake

Copyright @2021 by Chris Jake

All rights reserved. No part of this publication may be reproduced, distributed, or transmitted in any form or by any means, including recording, photocopying, or any other electronic or mechanical means, without prior written permission of the publisher, except in the case of brief quotations embodied in critical reviews and specific other noncommercial uses permitted by copyright law.

Table of Contents

vii

Introduction

Towards the end of 2020, Apple, in its usual yearly fashion, introduced a 13-inch MacBook Air with an Apple M1 chip. This device comes with the Big Sur 11 (2020) macOS, which is the latest Mac operating system.

What's the Apple M1 chip all about?

The Apple M1 chip is packed with a staggering 16 billion transistors, as it integrates the CPU, GPU, and all other important components onto a single minute chip. It is the first *SoC (system on a chip) for Mac. M1 chip is designed to improve the Mac performances as well as providing it with unparalleled power efficiency.

The Apple M1 chip allows your MacBook Air to provide up to 5 times faster graphics and 3.5 times faster CPU performances than the generations before it. Quite a massive improvement!

The new MacBook Air with the M1 chip is commonly referred to as MacBook Air M1 or MacBook Air (M1,2020).

In the exposition course, we will examine the latest features in the new operating system of the MacBook Air M1- macOS Big Sur.

Take Note

MacBook Air is often used to refer to MacBook Air M1, 2020 in this piece.

The Big Sur 11 (2020) macOS Big Sur: – What is New?

The new macOS Big Sur introduces a beautiful and nice new look to your desktop. The design features a translucent menu bar and Dock. More to this improvement are the updated alert notification sounds, updated icons, more spacious menus, full-height sidebars, and integrated toolbar buttons.

Notably, this new development delivers a more robust performance to your MacBook Air, making it faster than previous generations. It also features advanced technologies, including Thunderbolt/USB 4 and Wi-Fi 6.

Below is an overview of what macOS Big Sur promises to offer:

- **Redesigned Notification Center**

Your notifications and widgets appear in a single column. This permits you to customize your widgets as well as interacting with your notifications.

- **New Control Center**

The Control Center has a new arrangement, as it puts all your favorite menu bar items in a single place to enable you to access them as quickly as possible.

- **Faster personalized browsing experience with Safari**

This is the most notable improvement to the Safari app on the macOS since its launch. The macOS Big Sur presents a more improved Safari, which assures a faster-personalized browsing experience. You can add as many extensions to your Safari app from the App Store. You can quickly translate between webpages by clicking the translation icon (supports up to seven languages). Also, Safari offers a new privacy report that reveals how your privacy is being protected across the various websites you visit.

- **Improved Home app**

With the macOS Big Sur, the Home app now has several improvements. Some of the improvements include a visual status area giving a summary of accessories that requires immediate attention. It also features Adaptive Lighting for light bulbs (smart bulbs only), Activity Zones, and Face Recognition for doorbells and video cameras.

- **Spotlight**

Spotlight comes in a more improved and faster version. You can access high-quality suggestions even quicker, as it shows top search results and suggestions as you type.

- **Easier software update**

With the macOS Big Sur, you can now carry software update of your device with ease and quite faster than before. The updates begin in the background.

- **More iPhone and iPad apps available on MacBook Air**

See the App Store for more details.

- **More editing capabilities for Photos and Videos**

There is quite a much improvement in the editing capabilities in photo and video with more filters, special effects, photo retouching, captions to photos and videos, and many more.

So much more improvement is notable in apps and features such as Maps, Messages, Notes, Remainders, Apple Arcade, Family Sharing, Voice Memos, Music (Listen Now), and much more.

Read on to learn more.

Meet the New MacBook Air M1, 2020

> **Note**: The new MacBook Air (M1, 2020) come in three finish- **Gold, Silver and Space Gray**. The Silver and the Space Gray are slighlty more costlier than the Gold finish. Aside the price, the Gold finish slighly differs from the other two- Silver and Space Gray.

The notable feature of the MacBook Air M1 are listed below:

- It possesses an Apple M1 chip with an 8-core and 8-core CPU and GPU, respectively, and 16-core Neutral Engine. The Gold finish has a 7-core GPU.
- It comes with the Big Sur operating system (macOS Big Sur)
- 8GB unified memory configurable to 16GB
- 512GB SSD storage configurable up to 1 or 2 TB. The Gold finish comes with 256GB SSD storage and is configurable to 512GB, 1TB, or 2 TB.
- Retina display with True Tone
- Touch ID
- Thunderbolt (2)/ USB ports (4)

- Force Touch trackpad
- Backlit Magic Keyboard
- Bluetooth 5.0 wireless technology
- FaceTime HD camera (720p)

It is also worthy of knowing that the device:

- Possess a built-in 49.9 watt-hour lithium polymer battery, which powers up to 15 hours of wireless web and 18 hours of Apple TV app movie playback. Quite an outstanding battery capacity.

Take note of the temperature, voltage, and frequency rating to maximize your device:

- Operating temperature range: $50^0F - 95^0F$
- Storage temperature range: $-13^0F - 113^0F$
- Frequency range: 50Hz – 60Hz
- Line voltage range: 100V – 240V

More information on the device below:

- Date launched: November 2020
- Dimension (inches): 0.16-0.63-inch x 11.97 x 8.36
- Weight: 2.8 pounds
- Material: Aluminum
- Display resolution: 2560 x 1600 pixel

- Touchscreen: No
- Hard disk: No
- Finger Print Sensor: Yes
- Headphone/Mic Jack: Yes

What is in the box?

When you purchase the MacBook Air (M1,2020), it comes with the following items:

- MacBook Air (M1,2020)
- USB-C Charge Cable

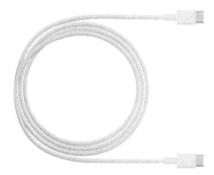

- 30W USB-C Power Adapter

Charging your MacBook Air with the power accessories

Your MacBook Air (M1,2020) possesses a built-in 49.9 watt-hour lithium polymer rechargeable battery. The battery recharges whenever the MacBook Air device is connected to power.

Here's how:

- Connect an end of the USB-C Charge Cable to a Thunderbolt port of your MacBook Air and the other end to your 30W USB-C Power Adapter. Before plugging the adapter into an AC power outlet, extend the electrical prongs on the AC plug; then plug it into a compatible AC power outlet. (Both accessories are included in the box).

Note: When your MacBook Air is off or is in sleep, the battery charges faster.

Battery's status

To check the battery's level or charge status, go to the right corner of the menu bar to locate the battery status icon.

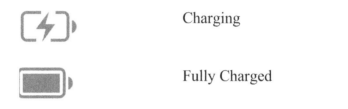

Charging

Fully Charged

Pro Tip: To check your battery's usage history over the past 24 hours up to the last 10 days, follow this path: System Preferences > Battery > Usage History

Tips for conserving battery power

- Reduce display brightness. (You can do this using the function keys F1 and F2).
- Close all apps while charging your battery to elongate battery life.

11

- While charging, disconnect all peripheral you are not using.
- When your computer is in sleep mode, disconnect other devices connected to it, as that could lead to battery drain.
- You can adjust the computer Energy Saver option from the System Preferences.

Familiarizing with The Parts of Your MacBook Air (M1, 2020)

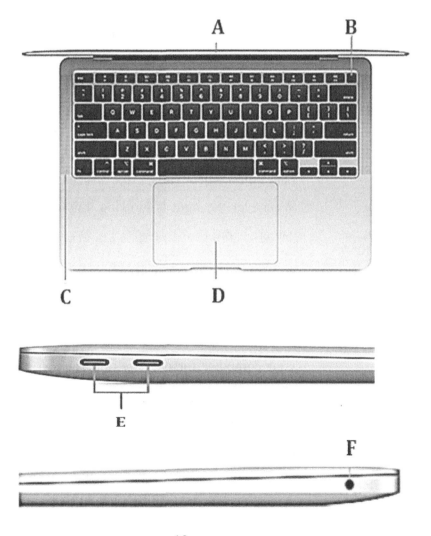

A. FaceTime HD camera

B. Touch ID/power button

C. Microphones

D. Force Touch trackpad

E. Thunderbolt/USB 4 ports

F. 3.5mm headphone jack port

A: FaceTime HD camera

The FaceTime HD camera enables you to make FaceTime video calls, take videos and pictures. Whenever the light is glowing, this means that the camera is on. (More on FaceTime)

B: Touch ID/power button

The button powers on your MacBook Air; press it to turn on your device or lift the lid. When you start your computer for the first time, or you restart the system, you will be required to enter your password; after that, you can set up your touch ID. The Touch ID can be used instead of a password to gain access to the computer, and it is useful for Apple Pay purchases. You can lock your MacBook Air by pressing the Touch ID button. (More on The Magic Keyboard featuring Touch ID)

C: Microphones

The microphones allow you to record audio and talk with people, thanks to the built-in microphones.

D: Force Touch trackpad

This is the home of the various gesture you can use to explore your MacBook Air. (More information on the trackpad surface shortly)

E: Thunderbolt/USB 4 ports: These ports allow you to charge your computer, connect to a display/projector, transfer data at a speed of up to 40 Gbps. These ports can be used to charge other devices such as your iPad, and so on.

Thunderbolt (USB 4)

F: 3.5mm headphone jack port: This port enables you to plug in stereo headphones or external speakers of 3.5mm jack.

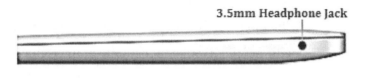

3.5mm Headphone Jack

How to use MacBook Air trackpad

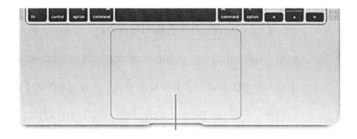

The trackpad gesture can help you do a whole lot of things, from scrolling webpages to rotating photos, zoom in and out of documents, and so many more. When you drag or try to rotate objects, you will probably feel a soft vibration when the objects are aligned.

Gesture	Execution/Action
Click	To click, press anywhere on the trackpad. If you want your click to be a tap, then enable *Tap to click* in the Trackpad preferences.
Right-click	Right-clicking allows you to open shortcut menus. This is done with two fingers, if *Tap to click* is enabled in the Trackpad preferences.
Force-click	To Force-click, you click and press the trackpad deeper. This is useful when you are looking out for more info about an item or icon.
Scroll	Slide your two fingers up and down.
Zoom	The thumb or any other finger can be used to zoom photos or webpages in or out. Pinch your thumb and finger open to zoom out and closed to zoom in.
Swipe	Swipe with two fingers to swipe left or right to flip through pages, documents, and many more.

Swipe between apps ↔ ↔ ↔	This gesture makes you switch from one full-screen app to another by swiping left or right. Use three to swipe.
Open Launchpad	This gesture enables you to open apps in Launchpad. Click an app to open it. *F4* on the function keys gives the same output.

Trackpad preferences/settings

The Trackpad preferences allow you to customize your gestures. You can learn more about each gesture, customize other trackpad features, set the click pressure you wish to use. To do this, go to *System Preferences*, and then click *Trackpad*.

System Preferences is the location where you can personalize your settings using of these two options:

- Choose Apple menu > System Preferences

- Click the System Preferences icon in the Dock.

The Magic Keyboard featuring Touch ID

A: Function Keys (F1- F12)

B: Touch ID (power button)

C: Function (Fn)/Globe Key

The Touch ID button serves as the power button as well, and it is located on the same row as the function keys. Below is a brief description of the special keys on the magic keyboard, as shown in the image above:

Touch ID/Power button

When you press this button, your Mac Air turns on. The first time of starting-up your system or carrying out a restart, you will be required to enter your password (if you have one). You can set up the Touch ID during the first setup; however, you can do it at any time by going through the *System Preferences> Touch ID pane*. After that, whenever your computer requests you to provide a password for access, you can place your finger on the Touch ID sensor to be granted access.

With the Touch ID, you can authenticate online purchases using your Apple Pay account.

- To turn off your MacBook Air; select Apple menu > Shut Down.
- To put your MacBook Air to sleep, choose Apple menu > Sleep.

Function Keys (F1-F12)

The function keys can help to access several system functions with ease. Below are the functions of the function keys.

- F1, F2: These keys are the brightness keys. Press to increase the brightness of the

screen and ☀ to decrease the brightness of
the screen.

- F3: This key is referred to as the Mission
  Control key. When you press ⊟⊔, you can
  view what is running on your system.

- F4 (Spotlight Search): Press 🔍 to open
  Spotlight on your MacBook Air, which allows
  you to easily search for something on your
  device.

- F5 (Dictation/Siri): Press 🎤 to activate
  dictation. To summon Siri, press and hold 🎤
  , and then make your request.

- F6 (Do Not Disturb): Press 🌙 to turn
  on/off Do Not Disturb. When the Do Not
  Disturb mode is activated, you won't receive
  notifications alert on your MacBook Air
  except you view them later in the
  Notification Center.

- F7, F8, F9 (Media Keys): These keys are used
  to execute media quick media commands such

as play, pause, forward a music track, movie, or slideshow. To rewind press ◁◁, to play or pause, press ▷||, and then ▷▷ to fast-forward.

- F10 (Mute key): This function reduces all audio output (sound) to zero levels either from the built-in speaker or the headphone jack. To mute all audio output, press the ◁ icon.

- F11, F12 (Volume keys): This function can be used to adjust the audio output volume either from the headphone jack or the inbuilt speakers. Press ◁⁾ to decrease the volume of the sound, while ◁⁾⁾ to increase the volume of the sound.

- Function (Fn)/Globe key: Press 🌐 to switch to a different keyboard. Based on your preferences settings, you can start dictation by pressing 🌐 twice. Press and hold the Fn key and a function key to trigger the command associated with the key.

Note: Each of the function keys can perform other functions.

Must-Have MacBook Air M1, 2020 Accessories

The accessories below are needed to help you connect your MacBook Air to external devices, and external displays, and many more.

- **USB-C to Lightning Cable**

This cable enables you to connect your iOS devices or iPadOS device to your MacBook Air for charging and syncing purposes.

- **USB-C to USB Adapter**

This can enable you to connect your MacBook Air to other USB accessories.

- **Thunderbolt 3 (USB-C) to Thunderbolt 2 Adapter**

This allows you to connect your MacBook Air to Thunderbolt 2 devices.

- **USB-C VGA Multiport Adapter**

With this adapter, you can connect a VGA projector or display to your MacBook Air. It also enables you to connect a standard USB device and a USB-C charge cable, which can charge your system.

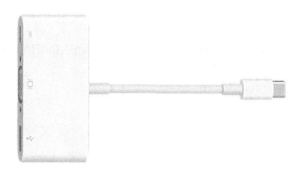

- **USB-C Digital AV Multiport Adapter**

This adapter enables you to connect your MacBook Air to an HDMI display. It also enables you to connect a standard USB device and a USB-C charge cable, which can charge your system.

<u>Note:</u> The Adapters discussed above are sold separately. Go to apple.com to purchase an accessory or any local Apple Store.

Using an external screen display with your MacBook Air

MacBook Air is designed to support an external display (screen monitor), HDTV, and a projector. This means that you can display what is on your MacBook Air on other screens such as a projector screen, another computer, an HDTV, and many more.

Connect MacBook Air to a projector or a VGA display

To connect a MacBook Air to a projector, or a VGA display, you need a USB-C VGA Multiport Adapter, which is connected to your Thunderbolt 3 USB-C port of your MacBook Air.

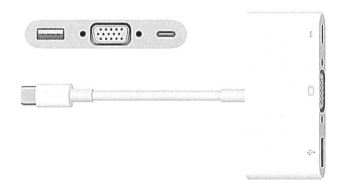

Connect MacBook Air to an HDMI display or HDTV

To connect a MacBook Air to an HDMI display or HDTV, all you will need is a USB-C Digital AV Multiport Adapter, connected to the HDMI port of other displays. In contrast, the other end will be connected to the Thunderbolt 3 USB-C port of the MacBook Air.

Tip: With an Apple TV, you can use AirPlay to mirror your MacBook Air screen display onto your Apple TV screen, provided you have an HDTV connected to your TV.

Note: The adapters and other accessories described are sold separately; they don't come in your MacBook Air box. You can get original accessories by visiting apple.com or from your local Apple Store.

Setting Up Your MacBook Air M1,2020; The First Setup

A Guide to Setting up your Mac

Welcome to MacBook Air (M1, 2020)!

If you start your MacBook for the first time, you will see something like this (as in the image above). The

Setup Assistant takes you through the steps needed to start using your new device.

Pro Tip: To use VoiceOver in setting up your Mac, press the Escape key. This is ideal for persons with visual impairment.

+ You will begin by choosing a country; this determines the language and time zone for your device. You don't need to complete all set up on the first attempt; you can skip some settings by selecting *Set up later* when such an option occurs.

+ You will be required to connect to a Wi-Fi network or Ethernet. This will prompt you to choose the Wi-Fi network and then enter a password (if required). If you are using Ethernet, you will choose *Other Network Options*.

Help: I can't find Wi-Fi status icon 📶 after setup

Solution: Open *System Preferences > Network*: click Wi-Fi on the list and then select *Show Wi-Fi status in menu bar*.

+ *Transfer information*: If you are setting up your new MacBook Air for the first time, you can click *Don't transfer any information now*. However, you can transfer your data from an existing/previous computer.

See *How to transfer your data to your new MacBook Air* for more info. (https://support.apple.com/en-ng/guide/macbook-air/transfer-your-data-apda75cd668e/2020/mac/10.15.3)

+ *Sign-in with your Apple ID*: If you have an existing Apple ID, you will be required to login with your Apple ID. Your Apple ID is linked with all Apple devices you use; it consists of an email address and a password. If you don't have an existing Apple ID, you can create one during the setup. You can also sign-up for an Apple ID from the link https://appleid.apple.com.

Note: It is recommended that you use the same Apple ID on all of your Apple devices (iOS, iPadOS, Apple Watch).

Help: I forgot my Apple ID password; do I need to create a new Apple ID account?

Solution: When you can't remember your Apple ID password, you can reset it by clicking the *Forgot Apple ID or password?* link in the sign in window.

+ *Store files in iCloud*: The iCloud feature allows you to store your content in the Apple cloud storage database. You can access your stored content anytime and anywhere. You can fix this during the setup, but you can also do that later by going through this path: System Preferences > Apple ID > iCloud.

+ *Enable Siri and Hey Siri*: During the setup, you can turn on the Siri voice command. More on Using Siri on your MacBook Air.

+ *Choose an appearance*: You can select how you want your Desktop to appear. However, you can skip this and do it later by going through this path:

System Preferences> General; select an appearance option.

+ *Set up Touch ID*: During the initial setup, you can add a Touch ID fingerprint. Follow the onscreen instructions. If you do not wish to add the fingerprint during setup, and you want to add it later, follow this path:

System Preferences > Touch ID > click $+$ to add a fingerprint.

Tip: You can add up to three fingerprints per user account and a maximum of five fingerprints for all your MacBook Air user accounts.

+ *Set up Apple Pay*: Apple Pay allows you to make purchases online without stress. You can set it up from the initial setup; follow the onscreen prompt to add a card, and the card's verification follows. (More on Apple Pay).

Apple ID: What you need to know about your Apple Account on your MacBook Air

Creating an Apple ID gives you access to all Apple Services. The Apple ID consists of an email address and a password. You can use your Apple ID to download apps from the App Store; it grants you access to Apple services such as Apple Books, Apple TV, Apple Music, Apple Podcasts, Apple iCloud, and many more.

To access the Apple ID control panel, go to *System Preferences*, click on Apple ID, which brings a list of items in the sidebar. You can access and update your account from here.

- *Overview*: This pane gives you the status of your account set up and what needs to be done to ensure all functions are working effectively.
- *Name, Phone, Email*: You can update your contact information (such as name, email, and phone number) associated with your Apple ID.
- *Password & Security*: You can change your Apple ID password here, turn on/off two-factor

authentication, generate verification codes to sign in to a different device, add/remove trusted phone numbers, manage apps and websites that you use to sign-in with Apple.

- *Payment & Shipping*: This option allows you to manage your payment method associated with your Apple ID.

- *iCloud*: When you select a checkbox next to an iCloud feature, this will turn the feature on. Contents stored in iCloud are not stored in your Mac locally. This will enable you to access the content on another device with your Apple ID and iCloud turned on.
- *Media & Purchases*: You can manage your purchasing settings and subscription to the accounts linked to Apple Books, Apple Music, Apple Podcasts, and Apple TV here.

Connecting with Wireless Accessories: Bluetooth Connection

You can connect your MacBook Air wirelessly to devices that support Bluetooth connection using Bluetooth technology.

- **Turn Bluetooth on/off**

To turn on the Bluetooth, check the menu bar to locate the Bluetooth icon ⚭ , and then click the icon. To turn it off, click on the Bluetooth icon again.

- **Connect to a Bluetooth device**

Once the Bluetooth is turned on, it becomes discoverable. To connect to a device, open the *System* list of available Bluetooth devices, select the device you want to connect to, and then click *Connect*.

Tip: A connected device remains connected until you remove it. This can be done by control-clicking the device name.

Help: I can't find the Bluetooth icon in the menu bar, what should I do?

Solution: Open *System Preferences* > *Bluetooth*> select *Show Bluetooth in menu bar*

Mastering your MacBook Air M1, 2020 Home Screen: What You will Find (The Desktop, Menu bar, Stacks, Dock, Notification Center, and More)

Suppose you are a new user of a MacBook Air M1, 2020 device. In that case, you must get acquainted with the Home Screen, as this helps you navigate your way through any aspect of the device.

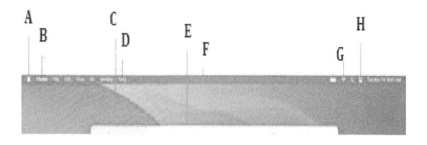

A- Apple Menu
B- App menu
C- The desktop
D- Help menu
E- Finder window
F- Menu bar
G- Wi-Fi icon
H- Control Center
    icon
I- Finder icon
J- System Preferences
    icon
K- Dock

Help: I can't find a pointer on my screen to navigate.

Solution: move your finger rapidly on the trackpad back and forth.

Apple menu

The Apple menu can be opened by clicking the Apple icon ![apple]. The Apple menu contains the most used items. This icon can be located at the upper-left corner of the Home Screen. Also, whenever you open multiple apps, the name of the active app appears in bold to the right of the Apple menu ![apple].

App menu

You can have several apps and windows open simultaneously. The App menu helps you find command in a menu that you can't find and checking the app menu lets you know if an app you want is active.

The Desktop

The most conspicuous and the biggest aspect of the Home Screen is the *desktop*, from where you can quickly access and open apps, organize your files, do searches, and many more.

Help menu

You can get help with your MacBook Air and macOS apps. You can type in your search keyword, and you can even choose from the suggestions. Also, note that help for your MacBook Air is available in the menu bar. You can access the macOS User Guide by choosing macOS Help from the Help menu.

Menu bar

The menu items change periodically depending on the app in use. The menu bar runs horizontally across the top of the screen. The menus on the left side are used to choose commands and perform tasks in apps. In contrast, the ones on the left are used to perform tasks such as connect to a Wi-Fi network or check its

43

connection status 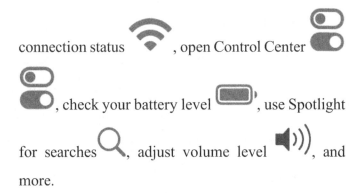, open Control Center

, check your battery level , use Spotlight

for searches , adjust volume level , and

more.

Finder

This helps you to search for and organize your files. The Finder can be used to organize and locate your files conveniently. Open the Finder window by clicking on the Finder icon found in the Dock. (More info on **The Dock on your Mac**).

System Preferences

This is the home of most settings and controls that you might want to carry out on your MacBook Air. (Read more on **Understanding the System Preferences on your MacBook Air**).

Dock

This serves as a convenient location to keep files you use frequently. (Read more on **The Dock on your Mac**).

Using stacks to organize files on your desktop

Using stacks on your desktop helps you keep files organized in groups based on date, tag, or kind. This makes your desktop well organized and clean. To access what is inside a stack, click the stack to access its contents.

How do I create stacks?

Click any space on the desktop, choose *View*, and then choose *Use Stacks*.

Alternatively, press Control, Command, and 0 to create a stack.

Another option to create stacks is to control-click the desktop and then choose *Use Stacks*.

How do I group my stacks?

Click on your desktop, and follow the path below:

Choose *View* > *Group Stacks By*, and then select an option on the kind of sorting you want.

Based on your preference, any new file you move to the desktop is automatically sorted into the appropriate stack.

The Dock on your Mac

The Dock can be found at the bottom of your MacBook Air screen. A Dock is a place where you can keep apps or documents you frequently use for quick accessibility.

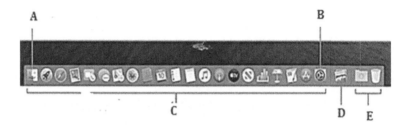

A. Go to the Finder

B. Open System Preferences

C. Apps in the Dock

D. Recently opened apps

E. Files, folders, and Thrash

Help: Can I hide the Dock from my screen?

Yes. Open System Preferences , click on Dock, and there you will find the option to hide it when you are not using it. You will also get the option to add or remove an item here, as well as adjusting the Dock size.

What can I do with the Dock?

There are quite several tasks you could execute within the Dock. Check below:

- Open an app/file

You can open an app by clicking the app icon within the Dock. You can also open an app by clicking the Launchpad icon first (which can be found in the Dock), and then click the app you wish to open.

Note: Apps that are recently used appear in the center section of the Dock.

- Close an app

You can close an active app from the Dock; all you need to do is to Control-click the app icon from within the Dock and then click *Quit*.

Note: Be informed that whenever you click the red dot in the left corner of an open window, the window is closed. However, the app remains open. An open app will have a black dot beneath it in the Dock. Check the image below for clarification.

The first two apps are opened while the other two are closed.

- Add an item/remove an app/item to the Dock

Whenever you want to add an app or item to the Dock, drag it to the Dock and place it where you want it to be within the Dock.

Note: Apps are to be placed in the left section of the Dock, while files/folders should be on the right-hand side of the Dock.

To remove an item from the Dock, simply drag it out of the Dock.

Note: Removing an app/item from the Dock doesn't mean it will be erased from your MacBook Air.

Pro Tips: On your keyboard, press ⌗ to open *Mission Control*. The Mission Control can help you view open windows and everything that is opened on your device. You can add the Mission Control icon 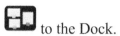 to the Dock.

You can modify the appearance and behavior of the

Dock. Go to *System Preferences* > Click *Dock & Menu Bar*

The Notification Center on your MacBook Air

The Notification Center can be accessed through the top right corner of your screen.

About the image above, click on any part of the encircled region to access the Notification Center. It is either you click the date or the time to open the Notification Center.

The Notification Center helps you to keep all vital information, remainders, and widgets in place. Get notifications from upcoming or missed events (messages, reminders, emails, calls, and more). You can also get details on weather, saved calendar events, stock, and more.

From the Notification Center, you can respond to an email, view details about a calendar event and whatsoever you want to do. Click the arrow located in the right corner (top) of a notification to view the several options you can execute as well getting more information about the notification.

The Control Center/System Preferences on your MacBook Air M1, 2020

Most of your MacBook Air system settings can be found in the System Preferences. The Control Center gives you instant access to the system control of features that are commonly used.

The Control Center on your MacBook Air

The Control Center gives you quick access to the features and controls most frequently used, such as AirDrop, Bluetooth, Wi-Fi, screen brightness level, volume adjustment, turning on/off Do Not Disturb mode, and more.

To open the Control Center, go to the upper-right corner of the screen and click .

If you wish to see more options for a certain control, click on the control. To return to the Control Center, click on the icon  again.

Pinning an item from the Control Center to the menu bar

Do you remember the menu bar?

You can pick an item from the Control Center and pin it in the menu bar for quicker accessibility in a single click; all you need to do is drag it from the Control Center to the menu bar.

You can also modify what you have in the Control Center and what you have in the menu bar. Go to *System Preferences* > Click *Dock & Menu Bar* and then select a control (on the left-hand side), and then click on either "*Show in Control Center*" or "*Show in Menu Bar.*"

55

Note: Some items cannot be added or removed from the menu bar or the Control Center.

Pro Tip: You can remove an item from the menu bar by pressing and holding the Command key, and then drag the item out of the menu bar.

Understanding the System Preferences on your MacBook Air

The System Preferences is the location to personalize your MacBook Air settings. You can customize your MacBook Air from the various options in the System Preferences .

How to access System Preferences

- From the Dock, click the System Preferences icon .

- Click the Apple menu , and then System Preferences .

Under *System Preferences* , there are several options to select from depending on your preferences.

How to Find Your Files Quickly: Spotlight on Your MacBook Air M1, 2020

With Spotlight $\mathcal{Q}$, you can search and find anything (documents, Calendar, events, messages, contacts, and more) on your MacBook Air. In addition, Spotlight Suggestions gives information from online sources such as web search results, weather, news, and other sources.

The Spotlight icon $\mathcal{Q}$ can be found at the top right corner of the screen. Click $\mathcal{Q}$, and then type your search keyword. You can open an app using Spotlight $\mathcal{Q}$ by typing the app name and then press the Return key.

Tip: To hide or show the Spotlight search field, type the Command-Space bar keys on your keyboard.

You can find Spotlight settings under System Preferences ⚙ where you can make changes to the Spotlight preferences.

Spotlight Suggestions

Spotlight Suggestions gathers information from various online sources such as Wikipedia articles, news, web search results, sports, weather reports, etc.

You can turn off Spotlight Suggestions if you want to restrict Spotlight searches to items on your MacBook Air only.

You can do the following with Spotlight:

- Get flight info: You can get your flight status and a map without using the browser. All you need to do is to input the flight number and the airline name in Spotlight.

- Open an app: To open an app using Spotlight, type the app name in Spotlight, and then press Return.

How to turn off Spotlight Suggestions

Open System Preferences > Spotlight: click to deselect Allow Spotlight Suggestions in Lookup.

Using Siri on your MacBook Air M1, 2020

You can use your voice to summon Siri to execute many tasks for you on your MacBook Air.

Siri can do so much for you, from giving you directions to a destination, send messages, play music, schedule meetings, modify preferences, and much more- all with a voice command.

To summon Siri to execute a task, say *Hey Siri,* and then make your request.

Note: You need to enable *Listen for Hey Siri from* System Preferences.
Be informed that Siri is not available in all regions and languages.

If you didn't set up Siri during your first setup, then you can set it up by opening *System Preferences*

> *Siri*; set your options such as the language, the texture, and gender of the voice, show/hide Siri from the menu bar, etc.

After Siri has been enabled, press and hold the Dictation/Siri button (which is the F5 key) to open Siri.

Note: When the lid to your MacBook Air is closed, "Hey Siri" won't respond.

What Siri can do for you

Getting things done faster can be made achievable on your MacBook Air by talking to Siri. Siri can do a whole of tasks for you in little or no time. A list of what Siri can do for you include:

- Set a timer
- Find and open files
- Play music
- Call a contact
- Find a location
- Provide reports on the weather
- Read news
- Translate a phrase
- Read a search result from the internet.
- And so many more.

On your MacBook Air, Siri can help you execute some task and answer some questions. Find out what Siri can do for you below:

Find answers to your questions: Siri can help you source information from the web, get solutions to some arithmetic works, get sports news and sports scores update.

You can say something like,

"Hey Siri, what is the score-line between Liverpool Chelsea game yesterday?"

"Hey Siri, what is half of a dozen?"

"Hey Siri, what is the source of petroleum?"

Translate languages: *Say something like, "Hey Siri, what is Thank You in French."*

Perform tasks with apps: *you can control apps with your voice using Siri. You can say something like, "Hey Siri, set up a meeting with Mr. John by 4 pm".*

Find and open files: You can summon Siri to find a file for you from your computer and open them right from the Siri Window. For instance, you can tell Siri to open the PowerPoint document sent to you yesterday by Ben.

Tips: From the Siri window, you can drag and drop images and locations into an email, copy and paste the text into other documents.

When Siri displays a web link, you can tap the link to get more detailed information in the Safari browser.

To know more about what Siri can do, ask Siri, "What can you do?"

*** You can't limit the ability of Siri until you have confirmed that it is not capable of executing a task you give to it.

Display settings for your Mac

You can choose a display setting for your MacBook Air based on the description below:

- **True Tone**: Using True Tone ensures that your MacBook Air matches the light in your surroundings. True Tone automatically adapts the color of the display in other to match the lighting condition of your environment to deliver a natural feel. You can turn on or off the True Tone feature by going through System Preferences > Displays > True Tone.

- **Dynamic desktop**: A dynamic desktop display helps you adjust the desktop pictures according to changes in your location's time zone. To use the dynamic desktop, open System Preferences > Desktop & Screen Saver > Desktop > choose a picture for Dynamic Desktop. If you want your screen change based on your time zone, ensure to turn on Location Services on your device.

- **Dark Mode**: You can use a dark color scheme for your desktop, dock, menu bar, and your macOS apps. However, your contents stand out in the background. This is very helpful to protect against eye strain at night when working on your MacBook Air.

Transferring Your Data to Your New MacBook Air M1, 2020 + Backup, Restore, and Update

You can transfer your files and settings from an existing PC or Mac to your MacBook Air. This can be done through a USB storage device wirelessly (from a Time Machine back up) or through an Ethernet cable and adapters.

Note: If your old computer is a Mac, you might have to ensure it is upgraded. Migration Assistant requires macOS 10.7 or later to execute this task.

Below are the available options on how to transfer your files:

A. Wireless transfer of data

During the first setup of your MacBook Air, you will be prompted to transfer data from your old device to the new MacBook Air using the Setup Assistant. If you missed this, you could do this later using Migration Assistant.

Steps

i.   Open the Finder window

ii. Go to *Applications/Utilities*

iii. Double-click *Migration Assistant*; this will take you to do a wireless migration.

iv. Follow the onscreen instructions.

Note: To ensure a smooth transfer of data from your old PC to your MacBook Air, make sure that the computers are connected to the same network and close to each other throughout the transfer process.

B. USB storage device files transfer

Using a USB-C to USB Adapter, you can connect a USB storage device to your MacBook Air. From the storage device, drag the files to your MacBook Air.

C. Transfer data over Ethernet

An Ethernet connection can be used to transfer data from an existing computer to your MacBook Air. An adapter will be required to connect the Ethernet cable to your MacBook Air. Before embarking on this process, ensure that your MacBook Air is fully charged.

More details can be found:

https://support.apple.com/HT204350

How to backup and restore your Mac

One of the safest ways to keep your files safe is to back them up regularly on your MacBook Air. Aside from iCloud, one of the easiest ways to do this is using the *Time Machine.*

The *Time Machine* is an in-built external storage device connected to your MacBook Air.

Files and photos in your iCloud Drive & iCloud Photos don't need to be part of your backup because they are automatically stored in iCloud.

Setting up Time Machine

Time Machine can help you to automatically back up all contents on your MacBook Air, including apps, music, photos, movies, documents, preferences, system files, and more. Time Machine allows you to restore your MacBook Air from a backup (Time Machine).

Note: Ensure that your MacBook Air is connected to your external storage device.

Follow this path: Open *System Preferences* 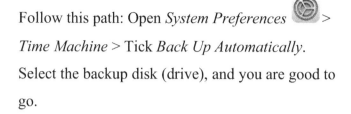 >
Time Machine > Tick *Back Up Automatically.*
Select the backup disk (drive), and you are good to
go.

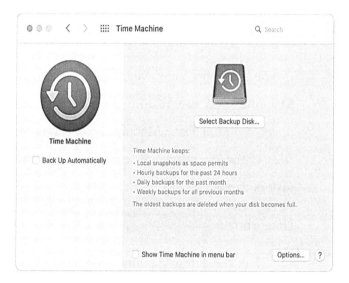

How to use another Mac as a backup destination

The shared Mac has to be on the same network as
your MacBook Air.

Steps

i.   Go to the Sharing pane of *System*
         Preferences on the other Mac, and then turn
         on *File Sharing.*

ii.   Add a shared folder, and then right-click (secondary click) the folder.

iii.   Choose *Advanced Options*

iv.   Click *Share as Time Machine backup destination.*

Restore your files with Time Machine

If you back up your MacBook Air using a Time Machine, you can restore your backup files all at once. With the Time Machine, you can recover your files if the operating system crashes or the startup disk is damaged.

Here's how:

-   Click the Time Machine icon from the menu bar (If not found on the menu bar, go through Apple Menu > *System Preferences* > *Time Machine*; select *Show Time Machine in menu bar*).
-   Choose *Enter Time Machine.*
-   Select the items you want to restore.
-   Click *Restore.*

Note: To recover your files from a damaged startup disk or operating system using Time Machine, you need to reinstall macOS on your Mac.

How to reinstall macOS on your MacBook Air

Your operating system files are different from your files, and having said this; they are kept separate in a sealed system disk compartment. If you damage a disk or completely erase it, it is required that you restore your macOS.

You may be required to reinstall a newer version of macOS or the original one that came with your device.

(Check How to reinstall macOS)

Update macOS

To know if your MacBook Air is up to date with the latest macOS, open *System Preferences > Software Update*.
You can select the option for automatic updates.

The Use of iCloud on your MacBook Air

The iCloud grants you access to your contents across other Apple devices. The Apple iCloud works with your Apple ID. Your contents (documents, contacts, calendar, apps, photos, and videos) can be accessed on various Apple devices provided you log in with the same Apple ID.

Turn on iCloud

If you didn't turn on iCloud during your first setup, proceed to open *System Preferences*, click *Sign In,* and enter your Apple ID. When you are signed in, click *Cloud* to turn on/off iCloud features.

How to store your desktop & documents folder in iCloud Drive automatically

On your MacBook Air; Open *System Preferences > Apple ID > iCloud > iCloud Drive >* Select *Desktop & Documents Folders*

Once this is done, whenever you save files in your documents folder or on your Desktop, they are saved automatically on your iCloud Drive, and this makes them accessible to you whenever you want to access them on other devices signed in with the same Apple ID, and with iCloud turned on.

Accessing your iCloud content on your MacBook Air

Your Apple ID is synchronized to an iCloud account, which comes with 5GB free storage space, which can be extended (premium). iCloud space storage is different from your MacBook Air internal storage space. You can access contents stored in your iCloud anytime and anywhere. Suppose you have other Apple devices such as iPad, iPhone, iPod, or Mac. In that case, you can sign in to any of the devices using the same Apple ID, and with iCloud turned on, you will be able to access any of your contents stored in the iCloud.

What else can iCloud do for you aside from storage?

- When you make purchases on App Stores, iTunes Stores, Book Store, and/or Apple TV app using the same Apple ID, you can enjoy them on all of your devices signed in with the same Apple ID.

- You can store & share photos and videos using the iCloud Photos and Shared Albums. To do this, follow this path: open *System Preferences > Apple ID > iCloud > Photos> Options*

  You will be able to share photos and videos with those you choose, and they can add theirs too, and comment.

- The iCloud feature allows you to locate your MacBook Air when missing, as you can use it on a map using *Find My*. You won't only get the location; you will be able to lock the screen and erase its data remotely. However, you need to turn on *Find My Mac*. How?

Open *System Preferences* > *Apple ID* > *iCloud* >
select *Find My Mac*

*For more info on lost or stolen Mac,

https://support.apple.com/HT204756

Pick Up from Where You Left: Handoff on your MacBook Air M1, 2020

Handoff allows you to start a task on a device and finish it on another device (iOS, iPadOS, MacOS). For instance, you can start typing a message on your iPhone and finish it on your MacBook. You can view a message on your Apple Watch and respond to it on your MacBook Air.

Note: The device(s) must be signed in to the same Apple ID and must have their Bluetooth and Wi-Fi turned on.

This is how it works

When other devices such as iPhone, iPad, Apple Watch, Mac are near your MacBook Air, an activity can be handed off as far as they are signed in to the same Apple ID and within the Bluetooth range. An icon appears in the Dock, and clicking on the icon activates the Handoff feature.

Note: To use Handoff with your MacBook Air, it will require an iPhone, iPad, or iPod touch with iOS 8 or later version and must have a Lightning or USB-C connector.

How to turn on Handoff on your MacBook Air, iOS, iPadOS device, and Apple Watch

MacBook: Open System Preferences> General > select Allow Handoff between this Mac and your iCloud devices.

iOS/iPadOS: Go to Settings > General > Handoff: tap to turn on.

Apple Watch: On your iPhone, go to the Apple Watch app, go to Settings, click General, tap to turn on Enable Handoff.

Handoff works the following apps:

- ✓ Calendar
- ✓ Contacts
- ✓ Keynote
- ✓ Mail
- ✓ Maps
- ✓ Messages
- ✓ Notes
- ✓ Numbers
- ✓ Pages
- ✓ Remainders
- ✓ Safari

How to copy and paste contents from your MacBook Air to other devices using Universal Clipboard

You can copy contents from one device and paste it to another using the *Universal Clipboard* courtesy of Handoff. The devices must nearby, and this can work within a short period.

The content copied on the Clipboard can be accessed across all devices signed in with the same Apple ID, and the devices must have Wi-Fi, Bluetooth, and Handoff on.

__Note__: You need an iPhone, iPad, or iPod touch with iOS 10 (or newer) or iPadOS installed, as well as the Lightning or USB-C connector.

Using Sidecar on Your MacBook Air M1, 2020

What is Sidecar?

Sidecar allows you to turn your iPad into a second display for your MacBook Air. However, you should be aware that you can only use Sidecar with an iPad that runs with iPadOS 13 (or later) and with models that support Apple Pencil.

Connecting your iPad with your MacBook Air

- Click to open the Control Center.

- Click , and then choose your iPad.

- When Sidecar is activated, the icon turns into a blue iPad .

Disconnecting your iPad from your MacBook Air

<u>From your MacBook</u>: Open the AirPlay menu and select *Disconnect.*

<u>From your iPad</u>: Tap in the sidebar of your iPad.

Note: Ensure that your iPad has Wi-Fi or Bluetooth turned on and needs to be signed in with the same Apple ID as your MacBook Air.

Extend your screen to your iPad

Whenever you connect your iPad to your MacBook Air using Sidecar, it automatically becomes an extension of your MacBook Air desktop screen. You can simply drag your apps and documents from your MacBook Air onto your iPad. To extend your screen, open the AirPlay menu and select *Use as Separate Display.*

Mirror your MacBook Air desktop unto the iPad

You can mirror your MacBook Air desktop screen onto your iPad screen, making them show the same thing. To do this, go to Control Center and open Screen Mirroring ⧉, and select *Mirror Built-in Retina Display.*

Using Apple Pencil

From your MacBook Air, you can drag a window to your iPad and start using Apple Pencil.

Learn more about the use of Apple Pencil on your iPad via https://support.apple.com/en ng/guide/macbook-air/continuity-sketch-and-continuity-markup-apdc0ae837eb/2020/mac/10.15.3

Connect to Internet Instantly: Instant Hotspot on your MacBook Air

Instant Hotspot allows you to use the Personal Hotspot on your iOS or iPadOS devices to connect your MacBook Air to the internet instantly without the input of a password.

Note: Your iPhone requires iOS 8 (or later version) or iPadOS 13 (or later version) to use Personal Hotspot

---

Tip: Use this link to learn how to set up your iPhone or iPad for Personal Hotspot.
(https://support.apple.com/HT204023)

How to Connect to your iPhone/iPad Personal Hotspot

On your MacBook Air, click on the Wi-Fi status icon

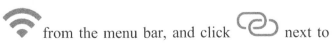 from the menu bar, and click next to

your device (iPhone or iPad) from the list of devices that appears. Once your MacBook Air is connected to your device (iPhone/iPad), the Wi-Fi icon changes to .

<u>Note</u>: If you are prompted to provide a password, it means you haven't set up the devices correctly.

Take note that your MacBook Air might disconnect from the hotspot whenever you are not using it; this is done to save battery life.

How To Take A Screenshot/Screen Recording On Your MacBook Air M1, 2020

From the Screenshot menu, you can take screenshots and screen recordings (including voice capturing). After taking a screenshot (photo) or a screen recording (video), you can easily edit, save, or share them.

Accessing the controls

To access the screenshot controls, press the key combination Command+Shift+5. You can decide on whether to capture/record the entire screen, a portion of the screen, or a particular window.

To take a screenshot of the entire screen, press Command+Shift+3

To take a screenshot of a selected area of the screen, press Command+Shift+4.

Taking a screenshot/screen recording

After pressing the keys to access the screenshot controls, use the icons at the bottom of the screen.

Use ⌞⎯⌟ to capture a selection on the screen and then click Capture to take a screenshot of the selected portion.

Click ⬤▭ for screen recording, and then click Record to start the recording.

Click *Options* to set audio options, modify save location, set timer before capturing.

Save, edit or share your screenshot/screen recording

As soon as you finish taking your screenshot or screen recording, a thumbnail appears at the corner of your screen.

To save the thumbnail, drag the thumbnail into a folder or document and quickly swipe to the right.

If you intend to edit or share your screenshot/screen recording, click your screenshot/screen recording thumbnail. To share, click Share ⬆.

How to Make Phone Calls and Text Messages on Your MacBook Air M1, 2020

On your MacBook Air, you can initiate a voice call, as well as receive a voice call. You can send and receive text messages. Be informed that you will need a Wi-Fi connection between your iOS device (let say your iPhone) and your MacBook Air, to make or receive phone calls.

How to make or receive a call on your MacBook Air

First, you will need to set up FaceTime for phone calls on your iPhone and MacBook Air. Follow the path below:

On your iPhone (iOS 9 or later): Go to *Settings > Phone*; enable Wi-Fi calling on your iPhone.

On your MacBook Air: Go to *FaceTime >*
Preferences > Settings; click *Calls from iPhone*

When someone calls your iPhone or iPad, click on the notification that surfaces on your MacBook Air home screen to receive the call on your MacBook Air. Your MacBook Air becomes the speakerphone.

To make a call on your MacBook Air, go to Spotlight, enter the phone number in the search bar, or apps such as Contacts, FaceTime, Safari, or Calendar.

Note: To make a call, ensure that the iPhone or iPad is in a nearby range with a cellular connection.

Sending and receiving messages on your MacBook Air

You can send and receive SMS text messages as well as MMS on your MacBook Air. Whenever you receive a text message, you can reply with any device within your reach, as all messages will appear on your devices (i.e., iPhone, iPad, iPad touch, and MacBook Air).

Using Apple Watch with your MacBook Air M1, 2020

Your Apple Watch can be used to remotely control your MacBook Air. It can unlock your MacBook Air automatically, and it can be used to approve a task that requires authentication.

Note: Your MacBook Air and the Apple Watch must be signed in to the same Apple ID, and the watch must be running watchOS 3 or later version. If you want to use your Apple Watch to authenticate requests, you will need an Apple Watch with watchOS 6 or later.

To use this feature, set up two-factor authentication for your Apple ID.

How to set up two-factor authentication for your Apple ID

Go to *Apple menu* 🍎 > *System Preferences* > *Apple ID* > *Password & Security* > *Set Up Two-Factor Authentication.*

Note: Ensure to select *Disable automatic login*

How to set up Auto Unlock

On your MacBook Air, Open *System Preferences* > *Security & Privacy* > *General* > *Use your Apple Watch to unlock apps and your Mac.*

What can you do with your Apple Watch on your MacBook Air?

Approve password request with Apple Watch

If your Mac prompts you to provide a password, double click the Apple Watch's side button, as this will authenticate your password on your Mac.

Wake your MacBook Air using your Apple Watch

With your authenticated Apple Watch on your wrist, you can wake your MacBook Air from sleep mode by just lifting the cover or by pressing a key on the watch.

Apple Pay: Make Purchases with Apple Pay on Your MacBook Air M1, 2020

With Apple Pay, you can purchase on websites using your MacBook Air. It is a secure and convenient way to make purchases online without worrying about your credit or debit card information being shared or stored by the merchant. When you shop online, look out for the Apple Pay button; you can complete the purchase using the Touch ID on your MacBook Air.

For more information on Apple Pay and Apple Card, visit https://www.apple.com/apple-pay

How to make purchases online using Touch ID on your MacBook Air using Apple Pay

With the first setup of your MacBook Air, you will be prompted to configure Apple Pay. This will enable you to use the Apple Pay button to complete a transaction by placing your finger on the Touch ID sensor lightly.

If you didn't set up Apple Pay on the first setup of your MacBook Air, open *System Preferences*, click on *Wallet & Apple Pay* to manage your Apple Card.

How to Share Files with Nearby iOS, iPadOS, macOS Devices with Different Apple ID

If you want to share files with nearby iPhone, Mac, iPad, or iPod touch devices that are not having the same Apple ID as your MacBook Air, there is an option for you – AirDrop.

Note: AirDrop can only work with iOS or iPadOS requires iOS 7 or later and iPadOS 13 or later, respectively.

Sending a file using Airdrop from Finder

- From the MacBook Air, go to the Dock, locate and click the Finder icon , click AirDrop in the left sidebar.
- When the person you wish to send the file appears in the window, drag the file to them.

Sending a file using AirDrop from an app

When using some apps, you will find the AirDrop option whenever you click the Share button ⬆️. This works perfectly with apps such as Pages, Safari, Photos, Preview, and some others.

When someone sends you a file using AirDrop, you can decide to accept it or not, and you can choose not to be discovered by other devices. The file sent to you using AirDrop can be found in the Downloads folder of your MacBook Air.

You can control who can send you items by clicking the Control Center icon 🔘, and then click AirDrop 📶, and choose either *Contacts only* or *Everyone*.

Note: Ensure that both devices have their Bluetooth turned on and are within 9 meters.

Receiving items on your MacBook Air using Airdrop

When you have an incoming item to your Mac from another Apple device using AirDrop, and you wish to accept and save it, click *Accept* and choose the location you will love to have it saved.

AirPrint: Print from Your MacBook Air M1, 2020

AirPrint enables you to wirelessly print directly from your MacBook Air to an AirPrint-enabled printer using a Wi-Fi network. The AirPrint can enable you to print wirelessly to a printer shared by another MacBook Air.

Printing to an AirPrint enabled printer

You can print from an app on your MacBook Air by clicking the Printer pop-up menu found in the Print dialog, and from the Nearby Printers list, you can choose a printer in the list you wish to print with.

Note: Ensure that your printer is connected to the same Wi-Fi network as your MacBook Air.

Help: I can't find the printer I'm trying to connect to

Solution: If you have your MacBook Air connected to the printer on the same Wi-Fi network, then try adding it with this process. Open *System Preferences>Printers & Scanners > click* ✛.

Section B: Apps Center

The MacBook Air M1 2020, by default, comes with some in-built apps. The apps are useful tools for your day to day activities. Explore them to get the best and effective use of them.

You can download more apps on your MacBook Air by clicking on the App Store icon , which can be found in the Dock.

However, some macOS apps are not available in some regions.

Search and Download Apps on your MacBook Air: App Store

You can download more apps on your MacBook Air by clicking on the App Store icon , which can be found in the Dock. Once you open the App Store, you can type in the name of the app you wish to download in the search field, and then press the Return key.

If you don't know the exact app you are looking for; you can type in a broad term like "App for weight loss," you will be given be a list of apps that are perfectly matched or closely matched to the searched term. You can browse through the app's categories to see if you can find apps that suit your needs.

Requirements

* An internet connection

- A signed-in Apple ID: To use the App Store, you must be signed with your Apple ID. If you have signed in earlier, you are good to go, but if not, choose Store & click on Sign In at the bottom of the sidebar.

<u>Ask Siri</u>: Summon Siri by saying, *Hey Siri, find apps for editing pictures.*

Some iPhone and iPad apps are now available on your MacBook Air. Suppose you have previously purchased such apps for your iPhone or iPad. In that case, they will appear on your MacBook Air if they Mac-compatible. However, you can search the App Store to see if such apps are available for your MacBook Air.

App updates

When new updates are available for your apps, you will see a badge on the App Store icon. When you click the icon, this will open the App Store, and then click *Updates* in the App Store's sidebar.

Apple Books

Apple Books allows you to purchase, read, listen to, and organize your library of books/audiobooks.

Note: Apple Books feature is not available in all countries/regions. You need to sign in with your Apple ID to buy an item.

Tip: You can ask Siri to help you find a book. Say something like: *Find books by Chris Jake.*

When you open Books on your MacBook Air, you will see a bookshelf where you can browse and search all the items in your library. You can choose a category to find new books and other publications from *Book Store* (which can be located in the sidebar).

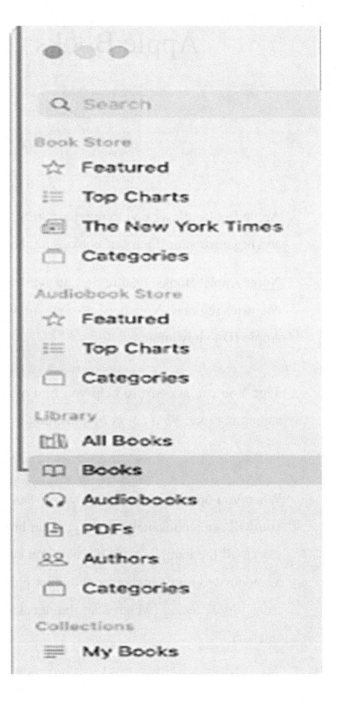

When you are signed in with the same Apple ID on your MacBook Air and other Apple devices such as your iPhone, iPad, iPod touch, you can access your purchased books, audiobooks, collections, bookmarks on any of the devices.

Switching your view to Night theme

Choose *View*, click on *Theme*, and then choose *Night* or click the Appearance button AA, click the black circle.

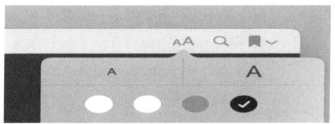

Note: Not all books support the Night theme.

FaceTime

What is FaceTime?

FaceTime is a Skype and Google Hangouts-like video telephone/video chat service that allows one-on-one video calls to be made on MacBook Air and newer iPhones, Apple iPad, iPod touch, Mac notebooks, and desktops. The FaceTime service of Apple is free of charge but requires an Apple ID and Wi-Fi connection.

Using the FaceTime app, you can make audio and video calls from your MacBook Air.

Note: To make or receive a FaceTime call, a Wi-Fi connection is required on your MacBook Air.

<u>Ask Siri</u>: You can say something like: *Make a FaceTime call to Chris*

Making a FaceTime call (Audio/Video)

Using the FaceTime app, you can either make an audio call or a video call. Enter a phone number, email address, or name of the person you want to call, then click the Video button for video call or the Audio button to place an audio call only.

To make a FaceTime video call, click the Video button ⬜, and make an audio call only, click the Audio button 📞.

Using FaceTime with a group

You can make a group call with up to 32 participants. To create a group call, enter a name, phone number, or email address, and then press the Return key to add the next contact. When you are done adding your participants, go to the bottom of the screen and click either *Audio* or *Video* to start the call.

Receiving a FaceTime invitation

You can join a FaceTime invitation, and connect with just the audio, video only, or both.

Tip: You can drag the small picture-in-picture window to any corner of the FaceTime window while a video call is in progress.

If your FaceTime video call is not answered, you can click on Message to send the person a text message.

Using FaceTime inside the Message app

When you feel text message isn't enough, you can reach out to a friend who has FaceTime app using a FaceTime audio or video chat from an existing conversation in the Messages app.

In the message window, click Details, then click the Audio button ☎ to make an audio call, or click on the Video button ▣ to make a FaceTime video call.

Screen sharing with FaceTime

To share your screen with a contact during a FaceTime video call, click Details, and then click the Screen Share button . Drag your files to the desktop on the shared screen.

You can make a regular phone call from your MacBook Air using FaceTime. This is possible when your iPhone is signed in with the same Apple ID with the same Wi-Fi network.

Also, ensure that *Calls from iPhone* is activated on both devices. To do this on your Mac, open FaceTime, choose FaceTime and go to Preferences, and then select *Calls from iPhone.*

Note: Your iPhone must be with iOS 8 or later.

Messages

The Messages app makes sending messages as easy as you can never imagine. With iMessage, you can send unlimited messages to Apple device users without any cost.

Start a conversation.

Make a FaceTime call, manage conversations, and share your location.

To use the Messages app, your Apple ID must be signed in. If your iPhone is with iOS 8.1 or later, you can send and receive SMS or MMS on your MacBook Air, must be signed with the same Apple ID.

Turn on Text Message Forwarding

To allow Messages link to your iPhone so you can send and receive SMS and MMS messages on your Mac as it is on your iPhone. Follow the procedure below:

On your iPhone:

- Go to Settings > Messages > Text Message Forwarding; tap your MacBook Air's name
- You might see an activation code on your MacBook Air, enter the code on your iPhone, and then;
- Tap *Allow.*

Managing group conversation in Messages on your Mac

- You can set a photo, Memoji, or emoji as a group image for easy identification.
- If you intend to mention a person's name in a group conversation, type @ before the person's name.

To see the options for managing a conversation and setting a group image, click the Details button ⓘ (located in the top-right of the Message window).

- If you want to get notified when someone mentions your name in a group conversation, open *Messages Preferences > General >* select the checkbox: *Notify me when my name is mentioned*.

Share a file, photo, or video in Messages

You can share a file, photo, or video by dragging them into Messages.

If you are in a message conversation field and wish to insert a file, click the Apps button 🅰, click *Photos*. Choose a photo, click it to add it.

Switch from Messages to FaceTime

From the Messages app, click the Details button (i) in the message window, then click either the Call button 📞 or the Video button 📹 to begin a FaceTime call.

Mail

With Mail, you can manage all of your email accounts from this app. It works effectively with most email services such as iCloud, Yahoo mail, Gmail, and many more.

How to add a mail account to your Mail app

Mail app allows you to sign in to multiple mail accounts in one app. Set up Mail with every mail account you have, so you can access them in one place-Mail. Select *Mail > Add Account*.

What you can do in the Mail app

- You can type in a keyword in the search bar to see suggestions for messages that suit or match your query.

- You can block messages from certain senders by moving messages sent from them directly to the Trash.

- Whenever you receive a mail containing an event, you can add it to your Calendar by clicking on Add.

- You can add an email address to your Contacts by clicking on Add.

- When an address is sent to you in a mail through the Mail app, force clicking the address will give you a preview of the location, which can be opened in Map.

- You can add an emoji to your mail, as well as photos.

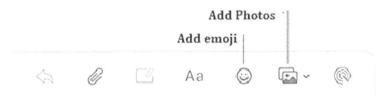

- Using Mail in full screen allows you to use the app in Split View, as this makes it easy to reference another message in your inbox even as you type.

- When you have unread emails, you will find the number of unread mails in the form of a badge on the Dock's Mail icon.

Find My

Find My can help you to locate your Apple device when missing or stolen. You can also use it to locate and track family and friends.

How to share your locations with your friends

When you open the *Find My* app, click on the People list tab, click *Share My Location*. This enables friends and family to locate where you are. You can share your location indefinitely, or for a day, or even for as short as an hour, and you could stop sharing your location with them whenever you like.

How to set location notifications/alerts

You can automatically send notifications to your family and friends when you are at a specific location or when you are departing the specific location. You can set notifications for when your family and friends arrive or depart a location too. You can view all notifications about your locations; go to the *People* list in the Find My app, click Me in the People list, and then go to *Notifications About You.*

How to secure and locate your Apple devices when stolen or lost

As soon as any of your Apple device goes missing, and you want to locate and protect it, you can do so by opening the Find My app, click the device to locate it on the Map, then click ⓘ to play sound on the device (in an attempt to find it). You should also mark the device as lost to prevent others from accessing the information.

Note: You can locate a missing device even if they are offline.

Music

With the Apple Music app, you can organize songs and albums purchased from the iTunes Stores in your library and the Apple Music catalog.

You can filter your content by Artists, Albums, Songs, or Recently Added.

Ask Siri: You can say something like: "Play a song by Bob Marley."

How to join Apple Music on your MacBook Air

Open the Music app on your MacBook Air >

Account > *Join Apple Music*; follow the onscreen instructions to complete the process.

As a new subscriber to the Apple Music service, you will get a free trial subscription, after which you will be charged monthly.

Note: Any music found in your music library and is not available in Apple Music is automatically uploaded to your iCloud.

Buying music content on the iTunes Store

Buying music on iTunes makes it yours; go to the iTunes Store in the sidebar.

If you can't find iTunes Store in the sidebar, go to *Music*, click on *Preferences*, click *General*, and then click *Show iTunes Store*.

To find Lyrics: Click to get the lyrics of the song you are listening to.

Tip: You can be doing other things on your MacBook Air and listening and controlling your music. This can be done by switching to MiniPlayer.

To switch to MiniPlayer, click , or select Window > Switch to MiniPlayer, or press Shift-Command-M.

Tuning to Beats 1

You can tune in to Beats 1 to listen to live broadcasts or listen to episodes from the Beat 1 family of shows. You can do this by clicking on *Radio*.

Streaming recommended songs from Apple Music on MacBook Air

Note: You have to join Apple Music to enjoy this feature.

You will supply some information about your favorite music genres and artists when you join Apple Music. Your preferences are used to make songs recommendations for you.

Using the Music app , you can do any of the following to find your most preferred music:

- To access the new music in Apple Music, go to the sidebar on the left, click on *Browse*, and then select a category.
- Go to the left hand of the sidebar and click *For You*; this reveals some categories such as *Recently Played*. The songs are based on recommendations tailored to you.
- To search for music in the Apple Music catalog, enter a keyword phrase for the music you are looking out for, and then click on

Apple Music found on the right side of the
Music app window.

When you find an item,

- Double-click it to play it.
- When you love a song or album, control-
  click the item, and choose *Love*; otherwise,
  choose *Dislike*.

How to download and add music items on your MacBook Air

Note: You need to join Apple Music to use this
feature.

You can add items to your music library from Apple
Music, which can be assessed on your MacBook Air,
as well as your other Apple device (iPhone, iPad, or
iPod touch), whenever you are signed in to Music.
As soon as you have added music to your music
library, you can download it to your device to play
offline.

Note: You can't burn music you download from Apple Music to a computer to a disc or added to another such as iPad or iPod; you can only download music directly from Apple Music.

How to add music items to your music library

- Phase one: Next to a music item, click the *More* button icon ●●●, next to an item, and then choose to *Add to Library*.
- Phase two: Hold the pointer and place it over an item, then click the Add button ┼.

Tip: If these options are not available to you, it might be that you are not signed in to Apple Music using your Apple ID, or Sync Library is not selected. To select Sync Library, follow this path;

Music > Preferences > General > (select Sync Library); click OK.

How to download music to your MacBook Air

After adding an item to your library, you can download the item to your MacBook Air.

- Click the More button icon ⋯ > Download. A faster way is clicking the Download button icon ⬇, which is next to the item you are attempting to download.

Creating an Apple Music profile on MacBook Air and its relevancies

Note: You need to join Apple Music to use this feature.

Creating an Apple Music profile enables you to share music with friends, but you need to add friends after creating a profile. The prerequisite to this is joining Apple Music.

Below is a step-wise illustration of how to create your profile:

- On your MacBook Air, open the Music app

  , and then click *You (*located at the left

  hand of the sidebar).
- Click the *My Account* button (The My

  Account button is like a monogram or a

  small photo icon; located at the window's

  top-right hand corner. Click *Get Started.*

Note: In *Choose who can follow you,* ensure to

select *People You Approve,* so you can share music

with intended people only.

How to add or remove friends from your Apple Music profile

- On your MacBook Air, open the Music app

  , go to the left hand of the sidebar, and

  click *For You.*
- Click the *My Account* button (The My

  Account button is like a monogram or a small

  photo icon; located at the top-right hand

  corner of the window. Click *Find More*

*Friends (*can be found at the bottom of your profile).

- Click *Follow or Invite.*

  Tip: To specify who appears in your friends' list, select *Account > Find Friend Settings.*

- Click *Close.*

Removing/unfollowing friends

To remove a friend from your profile list or to unfollow them, click the *My Account* button, click the friend profile, then click *Following* to unfollow.

How to accept or decline requests

Note: You will only receive requests if you select *People You Approve* during your Apple Music profile setup.

- On your MacBook Air, open the Music app

  , go to the left hand of the sidebar, and

  click *For You.*

- Click the *My Account* button (The My Account button is like a monogram or a small photo icon, located at the top-right hand corner of the window, then click *View Requests*.

To accept a request, click the Accept Request button or the Decline Request button to decline a request (prevents someone from following you).

iTunes Store

The iTunes Store is a repository of millions of songs, albums, music videos, and more for Apple device users to purchase.

Click on iTunes Store in the sidebar of the Music window to visit the store. However, if you don't find it in the sidebar, select *Music > Preferences > General*; check to see if iTunes Store is selected.

Note: Whenever you purchase or download music from the iTunes Store, it is added to your music library.

Signing in to the iTunes Store

An Apple ID is needed to sign in to the iTunes Store to make purchases.

In the Music app , select *Account*, and then click *Sign In*. Enter your Apple ID, then click *Next*.

How to purchase gifts from the iTunes Store

On your MacBook Air, open the Music app , click the iTunes Store. Click *Send Gift*, located below Quick Links, then follow the onscreen instructions. **Note**: The iTunes gift you purchase from a region or country can only be used for that country's iTunes Store.

How to Search for an item and a gift a friend

- On your MacBook Air, open the Music app

    , and then click in the search field and then enter your search keyword (The search bar is found in the top-left corner).

- When you have typed in what you desire to search, click on iTunes Store, located in the top-right hand corner of the window, and press Return.

- As soon as the results pop up, select the one that suits your search most, and then click on the price to acquire/buy the item of interest. If you want to gift the item to a friend, click on the arrow next to the price, which pops up a list, then select *Gift This*, and follow the onscreen instructions.

Click to buy an item

Click to gift to a friend, and more.

iMovie

You can transform your home videos into beautiful and stylish movie trailers with iMovie. You can import videos from media files already on your MacBook Air or other Apple devices such as your iPhone, iPad, or iPod touch.

You can use the built-in FaceTime HD camera on your MacBook Air to record video and then add it to your iMovie project. How? Check below:

Choose an event in the sidebar, and then click Import from the toolbar, choose FaceTime HD Camera, and then click the Record button.

How to create Hollywood-like trailers with iMovie

iMovie allows you to add photos and video clips to make wonderful trailers with animated graphics and remarkable soundtracks. To start this project, click the New button +, and select *Trailer*. From the Trailer window, select a template, and then click *Create*. You can add your personal photos and videos in the Storyboard tab, and from the *Outline* tab, you can add cast and credits.

Tips: Whenever you aim to stabilize a video to avoid shaky results/scene, from the clip timeline, select the shaky clip, click the Stabilization button ≡, and then click *Stabilize Shaky Video*.

Drag clips from the iMovie browser to the timeline of your project to initiate your movie's creation. Clips can be dragged into the timeline from the Desktop of your MacBook Air or the Finder.

How to add videos and photos on a MacBook Air into iMovie projects

You can use the Libraries list to add photos and videos to iMovie projects. From the Photos app, you can drag photos and videos in iMovie.

From the Photo app, you can access your photo from within iMovie. You can access this from the sidebar of the iMovie window and then select Photos. From the pop-menu at the top of the browser, click to choose a content category from the enlisted.

As soon as you locate the photo or video you desire to add, drag it into your project timeline. If you wish to replace a file, drag a new one onto the existing clip you want to replace.

From the Photos app, you can drag the photos directly into the timeline of your iMovie project. For videos, you will have to drag it from the Photos to your Desktop and then drag from the Desktop into the timeline of your iMovie project.

How to add sound clips to an iMovie project

Using the media browser in iMovie, you can use audio files from your music library or other locations using a media browser. From the Finder, you can drag audio files directly into your timeline.

If you wish to add a voiceover narration into your iMovie project, record it right into the timeline.

Calendar

The Calendar keeps track of your busy schedule, create, and manage events.

To add a new event, click ✛ or double-click anywhere in a day to add an event.

Double-click the event to invite someone, click the *Add Invitees* section, then type their email address to complete the invite. You will be notified when your invitees reply to your event invite.

Show the
calendar list.

Create a
new event.

Change the
calendar view.

Calendars +   Day Week Month Year   Q Search

Note: Your calendars are kept updated on all of your Apple devices when you are signed in to iCloud.

Tip: You can add a location to an event, and this will make a Calendar to show you a map and other information such as estimated travel time and weather forecast.

You can see more details about events in Calendar when you force-click the event.

Reminders

Reminders can help you to keep track of all your to-dos list and never miss an event. You can choose when and where you want to receive reminders.

The Reminder apps come with a smart list that automatically sorts your reminders into four categories.

Today: It lists your reminders scheduled for the current day, as well as overdue reminders.

Scheduled: This gives a chronological view of your reminders with times and dates.

Flagged: This gives reminders that you have flagged as important.

All: This gives a list of all your reminders in one place.

Tip: To mark a reminder as important, click the flag

icon .

Adding attachments to a reminder

Click the Edit Details button ⓘ to add an attachment
to your reminder. Proceed by choosing Add image or
Add URL. Alternatively, you can drag attachments
from other apps, such as from Calendar.

You can also group reminders by choosing File and
then New Group. Give the group a name you desire,
and then add more lists by dragging them into the
group. To remove, drag them out.

Safari

Safari browser is the built-in web browser designed for your MacBook Air. It is made to be much faster than the previous versions. It has a customizable start page that contains Favorites, Siri suggestions, iCloud, tabs, Privacy Report, and so on. Translation features are available on Safari, which enables you to get quick translations of sites in other languages, but the translation feature is not available in all languages or regions.

As soon as you open the Safari app, you can start surfing the web by typing in your search words or the website address you wish to visit. If the website you wish to visit is on your Favorites, then you can click on the website icon, and there you go.

How to customize your Safari app start page

You can show a photo as your background image on your Safari app start page or choose one of the preloaded background themes.

Click ⚏ to access the options to customize your start page. (The icon can be found at the bottom right of your start page). You can tick features you want to see on your start page and untick those ones you want to hide from your Safari app start page.

☑ ☆ Favorites

◷ Frequently Visited

☑ ◐ Privacy Report

⊘ Siri Suggestions

∞ Reading List

☑ ▨ Background Image

Adding extensions to your Safari app

You can add compatible extensions to your Safari app, as they help to improve the functionality of your browser as well as giving you a personalized browsing experience. When you download an extension, go to Safari Preferences, select the Extensions tab, and then click the checkbox for the extension to turn it on.

Note: You can get Safari app extensions from the App Store.

Open multiple webpages

You can open and view multiple webpages within just one window. Go to the far right of the tab bar and click ╬ to open a new tab, and then enter your website address or search terms. You can also press Command + T to open a new tab.

Pro Tip: When you hold your pointer over a tab, you can see a preview of the webpage contents making it easy for you to identify the webpage in the midst of multiple tabs.

Webpage Translation

With the translation feature on your Safari app, you can translate an entire webpage into your preferred language.

Note: You can translate between these languages only; English, French, German, Spanish, Simplified Chinese, Russian, and Brazilian Portuguese.

Safari can not translate all webpages for you, but whenever it is capable of translating a webpage, you will a translate button in the website address field. This tells you that a translation feature is available for that webpage as soon as the page is translated into a language of your choice, the translate button changes color .

Play your videos in Picture in Picture

When you are on a webpage playing a video, and you want the video to appear in a floating window in such a way that you can drag and resize it, then follow the procedure below:

- Click and hold the Audio button 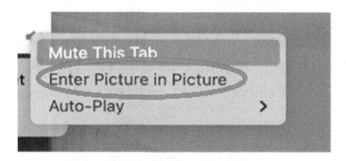 on the tab while playing a video.
- Click *Enter Picture in Picture* from the submenu options.

Safari Privacy Report

The Privacy Report button in the Safari toolbar gives information about the cross-site trackers that the browser is blocking on each website you visit and helps you understand how the website treats your privacy. You can access this information by clicking the Privacy Report button .

To get a privacy report, click .

Frequently Asked Questions about your MacBook Air

How do I check my serial number, operating system version, and name of my Mac?

- Ask Siri: Say something like, "What is my computer's operating system version"?

- Click Apple menu > About This Mac.

- If your Mac is turned off, you can check your serial number at the bottom of your MacBook Air.

Can I get support for my MacBook Air?

- Yes, you can. Visit

    https://support.apple.com/mac/macbook-air/

I am a new Mac user, and I just switched from Windows to Mac. What do I need to know?

- There are lots of tips guide in this book for you in switching between Windows and Mac. However, you can check the resources below via the link: https://support.apple.com/en-us/HT204216.

Can I get help with an app?

- Yes, you can. When you are using the app, click the Help menu at the top of your screen to get help and tips for that app.

How to Reinstall macOS

You can reinstall your Mac operating system if the recent one crashes. You can use macOS Recovery to reinstall your Mac operating system.

Since your MacBook Air (M1,2020) comes with Apple silicon, follow the start up from macOS Recovery procedure below:

- Turn on your MacBook Air (M1, 2020) and continue to press and hold the power button till the startup options window comes up. (You will see a gear icon with the label Options.
- Select *Options*
- Click *Continue*

Note: You might be asked to select a user, and you will be required to enter the administrator password.

Now that we have gotten to the macOS Recovery window, follow the step below:

- Select Reinstall macOS (name of the current version). In this case, it is the macOS Big Sur. Click *Continue*, and follow the instructions.

150

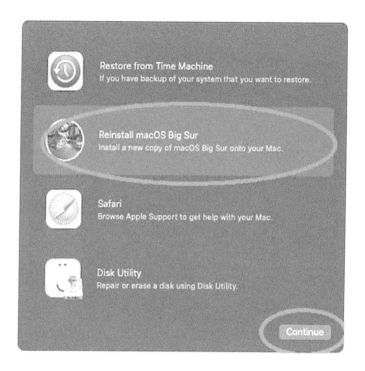

Installation guidelines:

- Do not allow your Mac to go sleep during the installation. Also, ensure that the lid is not closed during installation.
- Whenever the installer instructs you to unlock your disk, enter the password you used to log in to your Mac.
- You might have to erase your disk completely if the installer doesn't see your disk or if it can't install on your computer.

- If you are given options of choosing either from Macintosh HD or Macintosh HD-Data, kindly select the former.

Note: After the installation is complete, the MacBook might restart to a setup assistant.

Get to know your MacBook Air keyboard shortcuts

Familiarizing yourself with some key combinations will save you the stress of using your trackpad or an external mouse or device to do some things. Below are some keyboard shortcuts that can be used to execute some common tasks.

Shortcut	Information
Command + A	Select all items.
Command + C	Copy a selected item to the Clipboard.
Command + X	Cut a selected item to the Clipboard.
Command + V	Paste the content copied or cut from the Clipboard into a current location.

Command + Z	Undo the previously used command.
Command + Shift + Z	Redo previously "undo" command.
Command + N	Create a new document/ window.
Command + O	This opens a dialog to select a file to open.
Command + P	Print document.
Command + S	Save a document.
Command +W	This command closes the front window.
Command + Option + W	Close all windows of the app.
Command + Q	Quit the current app.
Command + Option + Esc	Force Quit an app.
Command + Shift + 5	Open the Screenshot utility.

Command + Shift + 3   Take a screenshot of
the entire screen

Command +Shift + 4   Take a screenshot of a
selected area of the
screen.

*** There are other keyboard shortcuts aside from the one listed above.

About the Author

Chris Jake is a seasoned photographer and a cinematographer. He is a freelance writer who focuses on the photography and documentation of physical environmental components. He designs wallpapers and screensavers for individuals and brands. He's passionate about sports and all genres of quality music.

Other Books by Author

Check out some books by the author that might be of interest to you. Here are his latest publications:

- **My iPhone 12 Mini User's Handbook**

A Comprehensive Guide for Beginners, Intermediates, and Pros in Mastering your iPhone 12 Mini + **iOS 14** Pro Tips and Tricks.

- **My iPhone 12 User's Handbook**

A Comprehensive Expository Guide to Master the Use of Your iPhone 12 + iOS 14 Pro Tips and Tricks

- **My iPhone 12 Pro User's Manual**

The Ultimate Guide to Exploring the Full Potentiality of Your iPhone 12 Pro + Exclusive Pro Tips and Screenshots

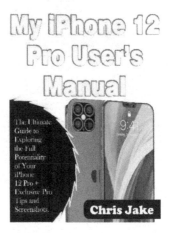

- **My iPhone 12 Pro Max User's Guide**

A Complete Manual to Master Your iPhone 12 Pro

Max Like A Pro + Troubleshooting

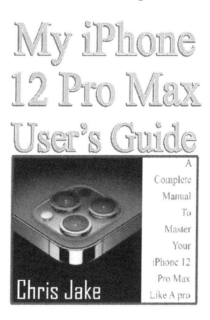

159

- **My GoPro Hero9Black Camera Handbook**

The Ultimate Self-Guided Approach to Using the New GoPro Hero9 Black Camera+ Tips & Tricks for Beginners & Pros

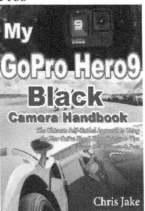

- **My GoPro Hero8 Black Camera Handbook**

  The Ultimate Self-Guided Approach to Using the New GoPro Hero 8 Black Camera + Tips & Tricks for Beginners & Pros.

You can search for any of these books online through Amazon by using the search keyword: "Chris Jake book on ......" let's say iPhone 12 Pro Max.

"Chris Jake books on iPhone 12 Pro Max".

Thank you for reading. Remember to drop a positive review if you enjoy studying this guide.

Made in the USA
Las Vegas, NV
06 October 2023

78684102R00098